River Scar

River Scar

poems
Paul Martin

GRAYSON BOOKS
West Hartford, CT
www.GraysonBooks.com

River Scar
copyright © 2019 Paul Martin
published by Grayson Books
West Hartford, Connecticut

ISBN: 978-0-9994327-9-2
Library of Congress Control Number: 2019935582

Interior book and cover design by Cindy Stewart
Cover artwork © River Scar by John Martin

for Rita

Acknowledgements

5 AM: "Cut Man," and "Sausage"

Big Muddy: "Aunt Vilma"

Commonweal: "Floating on the Lehigh," and "The Mower"

Floating on the Lehigh: "After Dark," "The Current," "River Scar," "The River in the City," "Staying Under"

Florida Review: "Hitching"

The Fourth River: "Stations of the Cross"

Here: "Abilene," "Falling Star," "Literature," "The Mulberry Tree," "The Pass," "Song Sparrow" and "Trexler Orchards"

Mad Poets: "Baseballs in Fall," and "Winter"

Morning on Canal Street: "Stickers" and "The Wren"

One Trick Pony: "Empty Bottles"

The Paterson Literary Review: "The Courtship"

Poet Lore: "The Boys on the Ice," "Building the Arbor," "The Cry," " Eating Steamed Crabs at Price's," "Leaving," "The Peach," and "The Pigs"

Prairie Schooner: "The Radish" and "The Shaking"

River Styx: "Laughing Buddha"

Southern Humanities Review: "Explaining the Urge"

The Southern Poetry Review: "Bread," "Cellar Goose," "Fig Tree," "Flood Baby," "Good Friday Afternoon," "The Key," "Passage," "The Trap," and "Tourists"

The Sun: "Dunkin Donuts"

Tar River: "The Cold," "The Mower," and "Sunday Drive"

Tifaret: "The Hawthorne"

I am deeply grateful to Steve Myers, Elizabeth and Brian O'Connor, Jim Murphy, and Rita, early readers of these poems, for their ongoing encouragement and their always insightful suggestions that greatly helped me in the writing of these poems. Thanks, too, to my brother, John Martin, for his cover art painting, River Scar.

Lehigh, first river,
wider and deeper
each year.

Contents

Stickers	15
The Peach	16
Magdalena Katerina Latak Polakovic	17
The Shaking	18
After Dark	19
Planting	20
The Pigs	21
Flood Baby	22
The Cry	23
Stations of the Cross	24
Good Friday Afternoon	25
Bread	26
Staying Under	27
The Pass	28
Empty Bottles	29
The Current	30
Cellar Goose	31
Trexler Orchard	32
Laurel and Hardy	33
The Boys in the Back	34
Leaving	35
Aunt Vilma	36
Hitching	37
Cut Man	38
The Trap	39
Building the Arbor	40
The Key	41
The Courtship	42
The Mulberry Tree	43
Huckleberry Picking	44
Baseballs in Fall	45
The Cold	46
Winter	47
Literature	48
Passage	49

Two Boys on the Ice	50
The Wren	51
Abilene	52
Tourists	53
Mother Daughter Arrival	54
Laughing Buddha	55
The Mower	56
Snake	57
The Fig Tree	58
The Hawthorne	59
Explaining the Urge	60
Sunday Drive	61
Dunkin Donuts	62
Walking the Towpath	63
The Radish	64
Eating Steamed Crabs at Price's	65
Floating on the Lehigh	66
Song Sparrow	67
The Red Fox	68
Falling Star	69
First Time on the Mountain	70
River Scar	71
The Tree Climber	72
The Giant Tortoises of Ironton	73
The River in the City	74
About the Author	75

Stickers

Only six or eight years in the world,
they were idling in the bright field
shaping stickers into a spiny wreath.
What entered him then?
Or was it a voice already in him
surprising in its rising strength
when he talked her into letting him
lower it onto her head like a crown?
When she tried to untangle it,
it moved beneath her fingers
deeper into her hair
and she began to weep, softly,
like an old, broken woman,
and he ran away to hide
himself in a windowless shed.
Now he can't remember
whether the punishment he expected
ever came, or whether they remained friends.
Only the distant boy, squatting
on the bare ground, his heart wild,
more thrilled than scared in the cool dark air.

The Peach

Sitting under the grape arbor, he unlaced
his work shoes, eased them off,
and leaning back, closed his eyes.
Small and ignorant as I was, I could feel
the heaviness of his body, beaten down
by years on the railroad section gangs,
too exhausted even to ask about school
and to tell me to eat those books
so I wouldn't have to slave like him.
In the shade's quiet, I watched
while he peeled and sliced a peach
left over from his lunch bucket.
Without speaking he extended a slice
to me on his knife, and I tasted
such warm sweetness, tinged
with the mineral taste of the blade.

Magdalena Katarina Latak Polakovic

Standing on the bed, I pulled
my eight-year-old self
 just high enough to stare down
the other side of the wall
at my grandmother bathing.
Looking up, she sent me away
with stinging Slovak words
that made me ashamed
to remember her in her nakedness:
her milky skin, her heavy breasts,
her hair, tightly bunned
for her life in the kitchen
and over the steaming tubs,
in that private moment unpinned,
falling loose and long down the back
of a woman I never met.

The Shaking

A strict man with black hair combed straight
back and a violet scar that flared

across his left cheek, he was opening
worlds to us, reading aloud

each Friday morning from Tom Sawyer,
Robinson Crusoe and I forget

what he was reading when he suddenly closed
the book, placed his index finger before his lips

and tiptoed down the aisle, our small classroom silent,
puzzled by what might be an unlikely joke

until he reached Buppa Darry's desk and lifted
him by his long blonde hair out

of his seat and shook him and shook
him hard, dropping him

onto the floor in a puppet-like heap.
The rest of the morning, except for Janine,

who raised her hand like a white flag,
we stared into our books, the words

drained of meaning, receding before my eyes
into a lost code.

After Dark

After dark the river rises,
submerging houses.
Fish swim through tall maples.
My mother's flowered dresses float
out of the closet up to the surface
of flooded Canal Street,
and my father drifts
from his bed out the window,
his black lunch bucket bobbing beside him.
From down in the columns of drowned light
comes a haunting song whose words
I almost remember
while a white horse trailing a frayed rope
swims up to the puddles of morning
where my mother and father say how deeply
they slept through the storm, how
they thought we had put away
the bat, the gloves, the garden tools,
scattered across the soaked, sparkling lawn.

Planting

Kneeling on a board over the shallow row
I've opened, I drop the tiny black seeds
of lettuce one inch apart, the way I was shown
by my grandfather when I followed his thick body
down the rows of peas, beets and carrots,
moving sideways on our knees, heads bowed
over the fragrance of freshly-turned earth
and sweat. I grew into a wide quiet.
I watched the seeds drip from his fingers.
Covering them and patting them down firmly,
he paused, his warm, round face slowly turned
toward mine, inviting me, it seemed, into a mystery.
Wordless, he used his finger to furrow the ground,
then poured seeds into my outstretched palm.

The Pigs

The boy sits in the dirt alley
between the back yards and the railroad tracks,
smoothing a place in the dust
where he draws and writes with a popsicle stick.
From the distance of years, it's hard to see whether
it's a circle or a girl's name he's inscribing on the earth.
He seems not to hear the voices of women
calling to each other across clotheslines,
nor the barking of the neighbor's chained dog.
It's the slow-moving freight that turns
his head in time to see their snouts
reaching through the louvered sides
of crowded stock cars.
Watching him, you can't know how drawn
he is toward their heavy animal presence,
their having to go where the tracks lead,
something going out of him toward them
as the train grows small in the distance,
what he'll mean when he says to his friends
he saw the pigs.

Flood Baby

We followed the receding river
down to its muddy banks, finding
messageless bottles, tires,
a few boards we saved
to rebuild our fort,
a shirt waving from a high branch,
a lone shoe filled with sand,
and among the debris, a naked baby doll,
sexless, that Annabelle carried home,
washed, dressed and pushed up and down
Canal Street in a carriage, a blanket
pulled to its chin. She told passersby
who leaned in for a look
how she saved it from the flood,
lifting it into the light
to better show the ashen face,
the wide, still terrified eyes.

The Cry

The only way home from school
was the bridge I approached, eyes fixed
on the far side where he stood, alone
and remote, rocking stiffly forward
and back for hours. *Shell shocked*
were the strange words my mother chose
trying to help me understand
what had happened to our neighbor's brother
on a jungle island halfway around the globe
from the quiet river town that watched him return –
gaunt, wordless, only that muffled cry
rising as I passed through the tight,
airless space between his lurching body and the fence,
my eyes lowered, books held close to my chest.

Stations of the Cross

Wednesdays after supper, the light growing longer,
my brother and I were called in from our play
to go to Stations and follow Him on His Way,
praying at the place where He first fell,
where He met his afflicted mother,
where Veronica wiped his torn face,
only women and a stranger stepping out
of the crowd to help Him, the faces
that ate and drank with Him receding,

leaving Him alone as Mr. Hlapac
those Saturday nights he came staggering
up the middle of Lehigh Street, falling,
slowly lifting himself, falling
again, his face bloodied
as he stumbled past us on our porches,
not one of us moving toward him.

Good Friday Afternoon

Between noon and three
no radio, no TV, no talking.
In the front room I sit
in an overstuffed chair
watching dust motes rise
in slanted window light,
trying to place myself
on that faraway hill where
Father Bermelin said He hung
by His nailed wrists.
But the intermittent shouts
from a nearby playground
return me to the quiet house
where the kitchen clock clicks
its slow seconds, refusing,
even for God, to rush.

Bread

"In the sweat of thy face shalt thou eat bread" —Genesis 3: 19

My father bends down and picks up the bread
fallen from the dinner table and raising it
to his lips, kisses it, and we go on eating
the pot roast and mashed potatoes he earned
from his work with spike hammer and crowbar
on the railroad section gang, "out in the open,"
my mother said, "with nowhere to hide"
from winter's blast and summer's scalding sun,
forced by his father from the schooling he loved
to give himself up for the family of eleven children.
His dream life of books receding, he rose
each day to the work, the lightning that bristled
around his shoulders keeping us at a distance
until the years ground him down
and he came through the alley toward home,
black lunch bucket in hand, an exhausted man.
Shamed by the old angers, he quit drinking,
tended a garden of flowers, became relaxed
enough to tell us his two funny stories.
What fire lived in him still flashed
when he exhorted my brother and me to eat
those books we brought home from school
as though they were food, better
than the meat and potatoes, the dark bread
passing from his hands to ours.

Staying Under

Trying to outdo each other we didn't come up
until our held breaths burst from our chests,
but no one stayed under
longer than those three brothers
the divers searched the river for
until the last one surfaced
half a mile south at the dam.
The whole town lined the sidewalks
as the three hearses passed, so long
and moving so slowly I thought of fish
idling, one behind the other,
in a quiet pool beneath my eyes.

The Pass

Walking the trail, I see the rotting ties stacked
along the route the Black Diamond once traveled,
connecting our dusty, tired town to the world,
as it did that day the three of us were settling
into our seats when the conductor appeared
in his dark uniform. My father held up to him
the laminated pass he earned through his work
with spike hammer, shovel and crowbar
on the railroad section gang.
My brother and I stared up at the conductor's face
as he studied the pass, then nodded, moving on,
the three of us easing back, unwrapping sandwiches
my mother had packed, the train picking up speed,
the trees and the river flashing past on our way
to St. Patrick's, Yankee Stadium, Radio City Music Hall,
my father's wide smile leading us
out of one country into another.

Empty Bottles

That last summer we went down to the river
we approached old Goosey's shack
secretly hoping the door was open
and Goosey lost in a piece of wood,
turning it into a birdhouse or another whirligig
that moved a small man to chop
the same log without pause on a windy day.
Quietly we stood in the doorway,
our eyes drawn to bare-breasted women
stuck on the wall above his rumpled cot,
their parted wet lips whispering
words we were close to understanding
when Goosey's sharp voice drove us out
to the path where we dawdled
a while, bored with kick-the-can
and building forts, not sure what to do
until we spotted the empty wine bottles
piled behind the shed and threw one
into the tumbling current, chasing it with stones
until we heard it explode,
then raced back to throw in another
and another, the water boiling
around each one.

The Current

Because the current was fast,
we started upriver of our swimming hole
and swam hard to the middle,
then let ourselves be carried
onto the smooth humpback boulder
rising above the water, basking there
in the water song and the sun,

but if we missed it, scrambling
at its slippery sides, the current pushing us
past, in over our heads and gulping water,
we learned to calm ourselves, to not flail,
to rise to one deep breath and begin
the deliberate stroking
toward the fast-passing familiar shore.

Cellar Goose

On the towpath one day a gray goose
flared its wings and charged at me as though it knew
I was the one who followed my grandmother down
to the ground cellar where she pinned a goose
between her knees, pried open its bill and forced
warm corn mash mixed with fat into its throat,
using her fists to move it down the long neck
into its stomach that dragged the ground.
When she finished, she stuffed
it back into the tight wooden crate
and we left it there in the dark
with its cold eyes, that seething hiss,
its liver already sold to the high bidder.

Trexler Orchards

Surprised by the big flatbed heaving
out of the orchard, churning up dust,
I recall the summer I woke in the dark
to catch the spine-jarring ride to Trexler's,
one of twenty or thirty white kids
among the Mexican migrants thinning endless
rows of peaches under a withering sun,
falling asleep at the supper table,
praying each night I'd wake to rain,
the brief taste of hard work
my father insisted would do me good
before I gladly returned
to school, forgetting the unseen ones
who followed the harvest,
shouldering their wooden ladders,
their hands like ravenous birds stripping
the trees of pears and apples,
bending low over rows of cabbages and potatoes
that stretched to the horizon, and reaching the end,
turned into the field again.

Laurel and Hardy

Saturday mornings he'd sit in his corner chair
watching Laurel and Hardy, laughing
so hard his face flushed red and purple,
his eyes tearing as he gasped for breath
until no sound came, his chest quaking
as though his ruined lungs were finally failing
while Stanley scratched his spiky hair
in puzzlement, and round Ollie rolled his eyes,
declaring *This is another fine mess*
you've gotten me into,
Stanley beginning to blubber and my uncle
dying, then rising with laughter
into the next Stan and Ollie adventure.

The Boys in the Back

Their suits wilted, reeking
of Saturday night's booze
and cigarettes, they stood in the back.

Once, when Father Matlos stopped,
threatening not to continue until they filled
the pews up front, they stood unmoved

and outwaited the tense silence.
At the first notes of the final hymn
I'd turn and find them gone.

Here they are, stones
apart in a silence deep and suspicious
as the one outside Halada's darkened

bar after last mass. Now, if only
I knew where to knock,
a door would open to clouds

of smoke and faces turning
toward the light, three of them in the far corner
waving me in, pulling up another chair.

Leaving

As though he were about to pray, my brother
brought together his hands, fingers folded through
each other, raised to his lips his lined-up thumbs
and blew through the narrow space between them,
short sudden bursts of breath that sounded
like a steam engine starting to turn
its massive wheels and pull a passenger train
slowly away from a station. Beside him
on the back porch steps after supper, I listened
to the slow, heavy choof - choof - choof pick up speed
as he blew faster into the furnace of his closed hands,
and I saw the train rolling down the tracks above the river,
thick gray clouds belching from its stack as it disappeared
around a bend, and then the high distant cry of the whistle
as it moved invisibly through the mountains, leaving
the two of us there on the steps in diminishing light,
the quiet of those left behind.

Aunt Vilma

Thin and hollow cheeked when she didn't
have her teeth in, she'd fire up
a Lucky Strike and wave away concern

as "shit for the birds"
and I could almost imagine the girl
stealing from her parents' boarders, running

away in the night, dancing on bars,
a brief marriage, abortion or a given up infant,
my older brother recalling with wide eyes

the time she flashed a tit at him.
"Oh, she was a firecracker, your aunt,"
offered old Mr. Turk, deep in his cups

at the Hunky Club, as though that explained the girl
who wanted more than that smoky factory town
even if she didn't know what it was

that night she spent sick and alone
in a bar until Leonard passed through
on his way to work and gave the owner money

for a room and a doctor, saying he'd pay
whatever it cost when he returned,
the two of them settling into a quiet life,

stopping by with her at the wheel
of the '54 DeSoto with its sharks' fins
to sit again at the kitchen table,

showing us how to blow smoke rings,
slipping between funny faces
and a sudden, faraway silence.

Hitching

Before twisted stories made me think twice,
I stood beside the road and raised a thumb,
waiting for a car to slow, stop, and ask,
as I opened the door, my destination.
Most times the driver, a gracious stranger,
saw in my young supplicant's face a chance
to help, and some easy conversation
to pass the time and break a long silence.
But more frequently than you might expect
I was met by a life suddenly bared:
details of a marriage's bloody wreck,
or nights spent dreading footsteps on the stairs,
those rides when distances slowed to a crawl
and the car grew close as a confessional.

Cut Man

The neighbor across the road was hit
hard by this last round
of layoffs, his pension lost,

twenty-eight years counted down
to nothing, and no union to stand up
for him the way my father did

when he came home from work
on the railroad section gang, ate supper,
then headed straight to his desk to file claims

for men used up by the company.
Hours later he sat on the floor
in the dim front room to watch

the fights in snowy black and white
from Eastern Parkway and Saint Nick's, smoky clubs
where hungry men, trunks splattered with blood,

beat each other into the canvas
for small purses skimmed by the Mob,
leaving them punch drunk out on the streets

while the cut man worked over
a fresh kid, a golden boy, packing the gash
above his eye with grease,

shoving smelling salts under his nose,
sponging him off,
sending him out for another round.

The Trap

Snuffling groundhog holes and pissing
on them, he lagged behind

while I walked the field, adrift in thought
until his frantic yelps turned me toward

what looked like a snake striking his leg,
which became, in my running toward him, a chain-

anchored trap sprung shut on his paw.
When I rushed in trying to pull it apart

he bit my hand to the bone, and I backed off,
wrapping my handkerchief around the wound,

and tried again, only to have him bite
my other hand, though slower

and less hard it seemed
as though he sensed my intention.

Cursing, lost for how to help, I remembered
the leash in my back pocket,

and used it to tie shut his jaws
and open the trap,

both of us finally freed.
My hands throbbing, I sat in the spinning field

and watched him race past the name
I was calling, into himself, into black dog,

one I came closest to knowing
down in corn stubble, dust and blood.

Building the Arbor

This first morning of June a friend and I are digging
six holes for the uprights, the air already close
as we take turns ramming the heavy crowbar down
through stone and clay, my friend wondering
out loud which ignoramus it was who said hard
work never killed anyone,
remembering his father's lungs thickening
with coal dust and me recalling my father's body sagging
under the weight of forty years of crowbar and hammer
on the railroad section gang.
Pausing for breath,
we declare how grateful we are not to have
to work like this for our bread,
then we raise the 4 x 4's and connect them
across the top with twelve-foot dowels,
stepping back to imagine the crossbeams
in place and the grapes, seedless Niagara
on one side, Concord on the other, climbing
through summers up to and over
the top, a green shade where we'll find
our fathers in the quiet of late afternoon,
unlacing their heavy shoes,
resting their pale feet on the bare ground.

The Key

for F. M., in memoriam

Almost asleep, I hear the clatter
of rain and think it's my brother
down there in the dark,
tossing pebbles up at my window

the way he did when he was out late,
missing the key I was supposed to leave
on the nail under the porch,
upset that I have once again forgotten him.

The Courtship

She was sixteen, in love
with the tall, blonde-haired guy
with whom she exchanged glances
as he passed her house
on his way home from work.
One afternoon, her parents away,
she invited him in.
That's how it started.
No perfume, no flowers,
no awkward kiss,
but her mother's roast pork
stuffed with garlic.
Oh, how he cleaned his plate,
she marveled fifty years later,
and how he asked for more.

The Mulberry Tree

Scrubbing purple bird shit off the picnic table,
I remember Mrs. Matusik cursing the birds
that splotched her freshly hung wash,
threatening to lop off the limbs
above the clothes line as she collapsed
a billowing sheet into her arms
and carried it back down to the cellar tubs.
Her husband sat in the shade
of the glossy leaves, sipping the sweet wine
he made from last year's berries
as he waited that June for his son's next letter
from burning Germany, silence
widening around him as he studied
the bees moving from stain
to stain in the grass around his feet.

Huckleberry Picking

for Kenny, our foster son

You'd have to know that ours
was the third family
he was forced to start over with,

that he rocked himself to sleep singing
about the lost yard where he played
with his brothers and sisters,

that we woke in the dark
and climbed the rocky trail to the top.
You'd have to hear the thin

plink of the first berry he dropped
into the deep bucket
and feel the slow hours

it took him to cover the bottom
and raise them, with help, to the brim
and see him lugging the bucket

down the steep mountain,
his purple mouth singing a new song
before he stumbled and fell.

Baseballs in Fall

for Humesy

He's torn out the tomato plants
darkened by frost
and begun his season of sighs.
Beside the bare garden he stands
in failing light
warming up with a few swings of the bat
next to a bushel of baseballs, the harvest
of a summer's mowing the high school field
where he stopped to pick one up and roll it,
nicked and green-stained in his palm,
sometimes gripping it across the seams,
extending his arm and snapping his wrist
before he dropped it into his pocket.
Now he sends a few line drives crashing
through the dry corn
before he finds the smooth uppercut
that drives them high into the cool air
above the field.
One after another he watches them climb
and drop into the wooded hollow,
pausing, letting his bat rest across his shoulder,
not sure whether to empty the basket
or keep the last one.

The Cold

This ten degree day in December I pull on
the gray thermal underwear my brother wore
on his mail route, the gray pensioners waiting
at lace-curtained windows for the blue uniform,
inviting him in for the warmth
of a quick holiday drink and talk
about the approaching storm,
the ripe scandal at city hall,
or their distant sons and daughters.
This was before the efficiency robots
started timing his route, the minutes
it took to walk a block, a supervisor spying
from a trailing car as he stamped blood into his feet
and laughed with them for a moment
they tried to extend before
he had to break it off
and keep on moving, a blizzard
of holiday catalogs weighing
down his pack as he started down the icy walk,
and they turned back inside, stranded
in another afternoon's long quiet.

Winter

With snow two feet deep in the yard
what better place to be than the kitchen,
the radio dialed in to the 50's station,
wine poured into large tulip glasses,
onions, garlic and mushrooms simmering
in a pan of butter and now Rita putting out a block
of Asiago, some olives and crackers.
When Jo Stafford starts singing "You Belong To Me,"
she pulls me away from the stove
into a slow dance, moving cheek to cheek
as we have for forty years. It's enough
to almost make me say I've grown to love winter,
but the truth is I don't want the future
rushing toward me. Let each day turn at its own pace,
darkness come early to the steamed windows.
Music playing, we'll sit across the table eyeing
each other, saying how much we like the pork cutlets
in Madeira mushroom sauce. Maybe tomorrow
shrimp scampi or that Brazilian fish chowder with saffron
I cut out of the magazine. So many recipes to soothe
these long nights: linguini with olive oil, garlic, anchovies
or with the marinara sauce we made last summer,
bringing it to a bubble while we set the table,
offering it to each other on pieces of dipped bread.

Literature

Pausing, the dental hygienist hands me water
for rinsing, and asks, after I say I taught English,
"You didn't teach literature, did you?" wincing
at the word and recalling the teacher who called on her
after each poem, asking, "What does it mean?"
causing her to throw up her hands in exasperation
as she does now, staring at me in disappointment,
as if I were the one who embarrassed her
in the classroom silence and turned her against poetry.
Before I have a chance to side with her,
she's bending over my open mouth,
picking and scraping with what feels like
a new determination and distance
in place of the easy way we had between us,
a warm, olive-skinned woman who told me stories
about her early marriage, her way of cooking
beans and rice, her difficult teen-age son
killed in a car crash, and how,
as he left the house, she almost
told him she loved him, her voice catching
as I lay under that lamp's full light with nothing,
really, to say, though I offered a few garbled words
that spoiled the fullness of silence.

Passage

In her last moments, my mother
sat up in bed, erect, slack-jawed,
eyes staring astonished
into a distance beyond us,
as though a mystery,
unveiled, were calling her name,
then lay back and breathed
and breathed, then didn't breathe.
Outside her window a clump of snow
fell from a branch and shook it.

Two Boys on the Ice

They've ventured past
the first tentative steps and now
stand in the middle
of the ice-covered river,
our eyes turned toward them
as we drive across the bridge.
It's the bright sun that has me
seeing tomorrow's headlines,
the adults shaking their heads in disbelief.
But for now they're held up by the ice, just
boys thrilling to an adventure, not
the ones who walked past the warnings
and dropped into dark water
that carried them past the only hole up.

The Wren

Did it fly in unseen
when one of us opened
and closed the door?
Might the cat have delivered it
lightly in the front of its jaws as a gift?
None of the window panes was broken.
Yet here it was, flying
around the unused bedroom, perched
in the wreath above the headboard.
We opened both windows to January's icy wind
and closed the door behind us.
Over lunch we worried
and wondered at its outsized song.
When we went back it was gone.
Sometimes it happens that way:
In a dark frozen time something enters
and sings,
unbidden and unexplained.

Abilene

for Marguerite and Mike

Without her knowing, he calls in a request
to the station that plays old cowboy tunes
each Friday night, so when the DJ says, "Now
here's a song for Marguerite from her husband, Mike,"
her confusion turns to surprised delight,
and he joins her in laughing and singing along
to the radio before he helps her up the steep stairs
into bed in the hard country of old age
and sickness, so distant from the endless, bright
horizons of those early years in Texas,
the fiery food and music and colors the song
gives back to her as she sings to herself in the dark.

Tourists

The restaurant deck overlooking the lower Niagara
is closed, tables and chairs taken inside
for the winter. The only one here, I stare
down at the wide, green river,
the swirling gulls, a fisherman's small outboard.
If you were with me, I'd tell you what I learned
from the book I was reading this morning:
that 11,000 years ago the Falls stood here
in Lewiston, its crest eroding
the seven miles south to where they are now;
that in 50,000 more years, they'll retreat,
foot by foot, twenty miles to Lake Erie and cease
to exist, numbers that might move us to silence
or my joking *I'll be an old man by then*,
this cold, wind-blasted gorge driving us
to a cozy pub where we'd settle in with the locals,
asking, as we usually do, about where to find
the best Italian, or a good beef on 'weck.
We'd reminisce about favorite haunts long closed,
and the city we loved, now in ruins—
in the drinks and small talk feeling the warmth
of one brief tourist for another.

note: 'weck refers to a kemmelweck roll

Mother Daughter Arrival
for Elizabeth's 50th

Outside the ice-scrimmed window,
a wind-buffeted dove stalls
and stutters in mid-air.
Puffed-up finches, chickadees, blue jays,
juncos, cardinals swarm the feeders
needing to eat all day
and save their singing.
In a spare season even the soul
recedes, surviving on patches of sun,
a stray piece of music,
seeming not to exist
until just now when it quickened
at the unexpected sight
of the two of you turning
the corner, the clouds
of your breaths commingling.

Laughing Buddha

Three weeks without rain, the vegetable garden turning
to dust, I water the limp tomatoes, the drooping
eggplants and turn the hose
on the laughing Buddha my friend gave me
one night without my knowing, placing it just
inside the wire fence that keeps out
the rabbits and groundhogs where he now stands,
both arms raised above his head in delight
as though I'm his long unseen friend,
his robe open, exposing
his huge, low-slung gut,
the water showering onto his bald head as he laughs
like some grotesquely bloated baby, joyful
for relief from the heat, laughing as he always
does, come bird shit on his round shoulders,
come blue skies and moonless nights,
come lightning storm, come ice,
laughing through no money,
through tooth decay, narrowing
arteries, lost chances,
laughing through the year
of my three friends' deaths,
laughing the wide, pure laugh
of someone who knows
something I don't,
or gone plainly mad.

The Mower

Down in the ground cellar
I'm showing Rita how to change
the water filter and replace the solar salt

in the softener, knowing she won't be able to lift
the fifty pound bags, saying she'll need to find
someone, and already I'm growing impatient

with this list prompted by three friends' deaths,
almost everything on it still undone—the living will,
the plot of ground, the complicated

money matters—so why am I now rolling out
the lawnmower, not even on the list,
showing her how to balance

herself and pull the cord, pulling again
and again harder, trying to swallow
the rising curses

as the engine sputters and coughs,
that second or two of hope
before it refuses to start.

The Snake

I didn't see it
until just before
the mower's blade passed over,
shearing off
its skin.

All day I kept
going back, hoping
it would live,

having crawled
down the dusty ages
from the perfect green garden
it never forgot.

The Fig Tree

The fig tree that died
back to its roots in last winter's sub-zero
has risen this summer to six feet.
Behind its lobed leaves
six small, green figs.
Each morning I go out with my tea
trying to rush them into ripeness
before cold winds whisper across the field.
Beyond the usual care, it's a matter of weather
now: a long, moderate fall and maybe
here, in a far outlying province of History,
I'll taste the fruit of the tree
that clothed Adam and Eve,
that fed the Romans and fattened their geese,
that heard the withering curse of Christ,
hungry for sweetness,
as he returned to seething Jerusalem.

The Hawthorne

Today, as we do each Lent,
Rita and I cross the field
to a place where the creek bends
and clip the bare Hawthorne branches
she'll shape into a wreath,
careful to avoid the long thorns,
stiff and sharp as needles,
quick to cut.
The dazzling white cloud
the tree will become
still chilling weeks away, hidden
in tight, tiny buds
at the base of the thorns.

Explaining the Urge

If you looked out the kitchen window and found me
on my back in the freshly dug vegetable garden
and came running, calling my name,
I don't know how I'd explain
what led me to drop the shovel,
to lie down and close my eyes.
To say I was tired wouldn't be true.
And how awkward to say that the fragrance
of freshly-turned earth called me past
the embarrassment of being seen
by you or the neighbor,
and to say what pleasure I felt sinking
softly into the loose earth.
Better to look up into your face
and apologize,
patting the ground to urge you down
to a closeness
that has nothing to do with death.

Sunday Drive

Adjusting the rearview mirror, I find my mother
in the back seat staring out the window
at the mountains, wondering what an acre up here costs,
saying we could build a summer shack.
My father, suddenly beside me, laments
the closed resorts and dying towns, all changed
since we last passed through here in the 60's.
Looking down at the map on his lap,
he grows excited, pointing out new roads
to try and admires the rest stop with its picnic tables
under a grove of trees I'm speeding past,
telling me to slow down, he can't wait
to unpack the ham on rye sandwiches,
cucumbers in sour cream, red beet eggs,
walnut and lekvar kiffles,
so hungry he is after all these years
for the rich food of the living.

Dunkin Donuts

It was worth getting out of bed in the cold dark
for an early doctor's appointment
to find this bright donut shop where I sit
with my medium coffee, cream and sugar,
light pouring in through spotless windows.
It was worth it to see the men's wide smiles
for the dark-eyed girl behind the counter
before they carried their coffee
to anonymous cubicles and construction sites.
To overhear the two gray pensioners
counting themselves lucky to have gotten out
just before the mill closed was worth it,
and to watch them settle in at their table,
steam from their cups rising before them
as they bit into their donuts
filled with jelly and cream.

Walking the Towpath

On the limb of a drowned tree
 rising from the canal
six turtles sun themselves.
The heron's a nearly unseen
stillness among the reeds.
Clouds journey across the glassy water.
The first lesson is to move slowly.
I try to understand the language
of the river by not trying.
The stone ground smooth
and round by the current
tells a long story.
I carry it in my pocket.

The Radish

Just the two of us and a gray old guy
behind the bar in the country hotel
my brother and I found after swimming
that afternoon in a quarry.
No television, no music from the jukebox,
we sat in the quiet of polished wood,
sunlit silver keys hanging from a chain,
a faded plastic rose beside the brass cash register.
So many years later, my brother gone,
the hotel razed to a weed-overgrown space,
I tell you, as we pass, about the summer day
we stopped here for a cold beer,
how, as the three of us drank in the stillness,
the humblest things were lifted
into the light, how I felt such closeness
toward my brother and the old man
slicing an icicle radish
he took from the cooler, salting it,
and offering, as a gift,
the crisp white rounds on a plate.

Eating Steamed Crabs at Price's

On a Saturday morning whim, we drive the back roads
past Amish farms and buggies down to Havre de Grace,
where we eat lunch at Price's, the ramshackle crab house
overlooking the bay, still here forty years after
we left, the wobbly table still needing a coaster
under a leg. The waitress who calls me "hon"
rolls out the heavy brown paper and we settle in
over the steamed crabs and pitcher of beer, remembering
our first years together and the birth of our daughter
after your long labor in the hospital down the road.
Glancing out the plate-glass window at sailboats,
we remember the friend who first brought us here,
writer, cook and painter, painting up to the end
the view from his hospice bed,
three years later his boat still in the marina below,
and we tear off the claws the way he showed us, turn
the crabs and pull off the aprons, then crack the shells
in half to expose lumps of white meat, licking
our spicy fingers, digging with knives
into the smallest chambers,
not wanting to miss one sweet bit.

Floating on the Lehigh

So I wouldn't forget even one of the sins
from the table in my prayer book, I wrote them down
and recited them from a notebook page

I unfolded in the confessional, squinting to read
in that tight, dim space, the priest straining to remain patient.
On the way home, my pocket burning with sins,

I ripped the page into the smallest possible pieces
and released them from the bridge, watching them
drift like confetti from high windows

onto the same river that washes over my pale body
this August afternoon sixty years later.
Called in as I stood on its banks,

I stripped and waded out to a deep pool,
dove and rose, lay on my back
staring into the dazzle of light,

a weight I was unaware of bearing
carried away,
as I floated on the forgiving water.

Song Sparrow

The song sparrow perched
at the edge of the fountain
dips its beak
and tilts back its head,
drinking twice more
before it flies into the maple's shade.

Three tiny beaks of water,
scarcely enough to be measured.
To live like that, needing
so little,
singing a pure song.

The Red Fox

When you told me I passed the dirt lane
into the cottage, I sped on
as though I had a surprise

in mind for the three of you somewhere
down that straight, flat road
where one mile of orchard looked like another.

That's when Elizabeth saw it up ahead
on the roadside, still,
its fur burning in last light,

its upright ears and pointed muzzle turning
toward our slowed approach,
small and vulnerable in the open

before it vanished into tall weeds.
It was August, dusk, the windows down,
Emmy Lou singing *We Shall Rise*,

the four of us silent,
staring into the weeds
where it left no path.

Falling Star

It streaked out of the southern horizon
and when it passed above the house
we ran from the front porch
to the back just in time to see
it crossing the field
and go dark.

I didn't dream it, did I—the summer night,
a star falling across the sky,
you and me, the child,
now grown and gone, looking up?

First Time on the Mountain

One of the old Slovaks now, he sits
on a park bench in his battered hat, staring
across Delaware Avenue at the stores, shoppers,
and above them at the looming mountain,
remembering the steep, stony climb to the top
in first light, the elation of looking down
on the river and town,
the discouraging sound of the first huckleberries
hitting the bottom of the water bucket.
How careful he was, before he reached, to look
for the snakes old timers warned about.
Slowly the berries rose and he stopped to eat
his sandwich, staring down at the town to find
his house, school, playground, and a single car
he could follow down Delaware
and through each turn in the gridwork
of streets and miniature houses,
the world he descended to,
bearing as a gift the brimming blue bucket.

River Scar

The first summer I waded into the river
I stepped on a piece of glass
and an older girl carried me home
on her back.

Tonight, before I rolled into bed
I searched for the scar, my first,
receded through sixty years
and invisible now,
though I still feel it
deep in my heel.

The Tree Climber

The tall maple stands in place and sways
in thunder, lightning, torrents of rain.
What calls me in my old age to chance
a climb high into its limbs
and look down on the house
as I did when a boy on Canal Street
under a black crackling sky, a stinging rain,
hugging a wind-tossed limb inside
the heaving tree's branches closing and opening
so the neighbor woman taking down her wash
looked up at me, half naked, and said nothing,
went running for no one,
as though it were my natural place,
the wild one, the one I heard her say
should have his head examined.

The Giant Tortoises of Ironton

The huge stones
in the neighbor's green lawn
have withdrawn their heads and legs
under their grey-black shells.
Among the suburban houses
they rest,
gathering their shallow breaths
before they lift
themselves and continue
plodding through the ages, leaving
deep impressions in the grass.

The River in the City

How strange to see the river here
in the city, far from the green
country of long summers and swimming.

If only I could reach down
and touch it, let it shape
itself around my wrist

so as to remember me
as it moves under the dark bridge
past the looming blast furnaces.

About the Author

Paul Martin's poems have appeared in *America, Boulevard, Commonweal, New Letters, Poet Lore, Poetry East, River Styx, The Southern Poetry Review, The Sun*. His first book, *Closing Distances*, was published by The Backwaters Press. He has published six chapbooks, three of them prize winners: *Rooms of the Living* was a co-winner of the Autumn House Press Chapbook Prize, *Floating on the Lehigh* won the 2015 Grayson Books Chapbook Contest, and *Mourning Dove* won Comstock Review's Jessie Bryce Niles Chapbook Prize. His poems have appeared on Writer's Almanac, Poetry Daily, in Ted Kooser's American Life in Poetry and numerous anthologies. His poem, "The Radish," won Prairie Schooner's Glenna Luschei Poetry Prize. He has twice been awarded poetry fellowships from the PA Council on the Arts.

www.ingramcontent.com/pod-product-compliance
Lightning Source LLC
Chambersburg PA
CBHW050446010526
44118CB00013B/1697